1

ISBN : 9798883002426

TABLE OF CONTENTS

Breakfast 0 Point Weight Loss Meals

| Muffin Tin Eggs

Prep Time	Cook Time	Calories
10 min	40 min	172 kcal

| Ingredients :

- 12 eggs
- 1 teaspoon Montreal Steak Seasoning Blend
- AD
- 1 red, orange, or green pepper, diced
- ½ pound 99% fat-free ground turkey breast
- ½ teaspoon sage
- ½ teaspoon salt
- ½ teaspoon black pepper
- ¼ teaspoon red pepper flakes
- ¼ teaspoon marjoram
- Non-Stick Cooking Spray

| Instructions :

1. Preheat oven to 350 degrees.

2. Spray a muffin tin with non-stick spray.

3. Spray a large non-stick skillet with non-stick spray. On medium heat cook ground turkey, sage, salt, black pepper, red pepper flakes, and marjoram for 7-10 minutes or until cooked through. Stir consistently to prevent sticking.

4. While turkey is cooking, in a large bowl, beat eggs and Montreal steak seasoning together until well mixed and fluffy (2-3 minutes). Stir in diced bell pepper.

5. Once the turkey is cooked through, spoon into the muffin tins spreading equally between each muffin tin.

6. Pour egg mixture over the turkey filling ¾ of the way full.

7. Bake at 350 degrees for 30 minutes.

Per serving: CALORIES: 172, TOTAL FAT: 9.2g, SATURATED FAT: 2.7g, CHOLESTEROL: 351mg, SODIUM: 462mg, CARBOHYDRATES: 1.8g, FIBER: .4g, SUGAR: 1.2g, PROTEIN: 20.7g

| Healthy Pancake and French Toast Topping

Calories

53 kcal

| Ingredients :
- 1 ripe banana
- 1/4 teaspoon vanilla
- ground cinnamon

| Instructions :

1. Cut the banana in half and mash 1/2 of it in a small microwave proof bowl.
2. Slice the other half and add to mashed banana.
3. Heat in microwave on high for 30 seconds.
4. Mix in vanilla and add a few dashes of cinnamon.
5. Use immediately (or it will turn brown).

Per serving: For one serving (two in recipe): 53 calories, 0.2 g fat, 0.0 g saturated fat, 13.5 g carbohydrates, 7.2 g sugar, 0.6 g protein, 1.5 g fiber, 1 mg sodium, 0 Freestyle SmartPts

| Blueberry FroYo Bark

Prep Time

10 min

| Ingredients :

- 1 cup non-fat plain Greek yogurt
- 1 teaspoon vanilla extract
- 2 packets Splenda
- 4-6 strawberries
- 1 teaspoon cocoa powder (optional)

| Instructions :

1. In a small bowl, mix the yogurt, vanilla and Splenda.

2. Line an 8 x 8 baking pan with parchment paper. Pour the yogurt mixture into the pan evenly.

3. Cut up the strawberries and add them to the yogurt. I pushed them into the yogurt slightly.

4. Add the cocoa powder using a mesh strainer.

5. Freeze for 2 hours.

Fried Egg Turkey "Sandwich"

Ingredients :

- 2 or 3 ounces of ground turkey
- 1 large egg
- Romaine lettuce leaves
- Salt and pepper to taste.

Instructions :

1. Liberally coat a large skillet with 0 calorie cooking spray
2. Make two small, thin patties out of the ground turkey
3. Fry the patties on both sides until brown (about 3 minutes on each side)
4. Spray the pan again and fry the egg, turning once
5. Put the egg in the middle of the patties, along with salt, pepper, and any other spice you might like to add.
6. Wrap in romaine lettuce leaves just before eating.

| Crustless Frittatas

Prep Time	**Cook Time**
10 min	**20 min**

| Ingredients :

- 1 cup peppers and onions vegetable mix 0 Points
- 1 cup cooked mushroom pieces 0 Points
- 1 cup cooked spinach 0 Points

- 1 cup broccoli slaw 0 Points
- 8 eggs 0 Points
- 1/4 second spray Pam Cooking Spray, No-Stick, Olive Oil 0 Points
- 1 tsp black pepper 0 Points.

| Instructions :

1. Spray a pan with Pam cooking spray no-stick olive oil
2. Sautee Onions, peppers, mushrooms, spinach and broccoli slaw till browned.
3. Transfer mixture to a pie pan
4. Add 8 beaten eggs on top and bake for twenty minutes at 350
5. Add pepper to taste

Per serving: Serves four - o points per serving

Southwest Black Bean Egg Muffins

Prep Time	Cook Time	Calories
10 min	**20 min**	**151 kcal**

Ingredients :

- 1.5 cups canned black beans, drained and rinsed
- 1 green bell pepper, diced
- 1 jalapeno, seeded and diced
- 1/2 cup red onion, diced
- 8 large eggs
- Salt and pepper

Instructions :

1. Preheat the oven to 350 degrees.

2. Spray a nonstick skillet with cooking spray. Add the peppers, onion, and jalapeno if using and cook until tender, about 6-8 minutes.

3. Meanwhile, whisk together the eggs. Season with salt and pepper.

4. Add the peppers, onions, and black beans to the eggs.

5. Spray a muffin tin with cooking spray. Pour in the egg mixture.

6. Bake for 20-25 minutes until puffed up and cooked through.

Per serving:	Polyunsaturated	**Total**
Total Fat 7g	Fat 0g	**Carbohydrate** 13g
10%	**Cholesterol** 248m	4%
Saturated Fat 2g	g	Dietary Fiber 5g
11%	83%	19%
Monounsaturated	**Sodium** 326mg	Sugars 2g
Fat 0g	14%	**Protein** 12g

| Very Berry Smoothie

| Ingredients :

- 1/2 cup
  fresh raspberries berries

- 1/2 cup fresh strawberries

- 1/4 cup fresh blueberries

- 1 cup ice

- 1/2 cup almond milk

- 1/4 cup fat free plain greek yogurt

- 1/2 tsp cinnamon (optional)

| Instructions :

1. Dump all ingredients into a blender

2. Blend

3. Pour in a cup and enjoy!

| Tofu Scramble

Calories

105 kcal

| Ingredients :

- 1 package extra firm tofu
- 3 scallions, chopped (optional)
- 2 teaspoons curry powder
- 1 teaspoon ground cumin non-stick spray.

| Instructions :

1. Heat a non-stick pan over medium high heat and spray with non-stick spray.

2. Crumble tofu into pan and add scallions.

3. Heat (stirring often) for 8 minutes until most of the water has steamed out.

4. Mix in the curry powder and cumin.

5. If mixture is too dry add a little water back in to get to desired consistency.

Per serving: 105 calories, 6 g fat, 0.6 g saturated fat, 6.9 g carbohydrates, 1.1 g sugar, 9.3 g protein, 2.9 g fiber, 25 mg sodium, 0 Freestyle SmartPts

| Salsa and Vegetable Egg Scramble

| Ingredients :

- 2 Eggs
- ½ tsp salt and pepper to taste
- 2 to 3 tablespoons of non-fat salsa
- ½ cup of vegetables of your choosing
- Non fat cooking spray.

| Instructions :

1. Whisk eggs in a small bowl. Add chopped vegetables of your choice (think onions, bell peppers, zucchini, broccoli, cilantro, chives, etc.) and spices.

2. Mix well

3. Spray non-stick pan liberally with non fat cooking spray.

4. Cook egg mixture over medium flame until vegetables are tender and eggs are cooked.

5. Place eggs on plate and top with salsa.

Chicken Breakfast Sausage

Prep Time	Cook Time
5 min	**6 min**

Ingredients :

- 1 pound ground chicken breast
- 1 teaspoon sage
- 1 teaspoon garlic powder
- 1 teaspoon onion powder
- 1 teaspoon black pepper
- 1 teaspoon paprika
- ½ teaspoon fennel
- ½ teaspoon salt
- ½ teaspoon cumin.

Instructions :

1. Spray nonstick skillet with nonstick cooking spray
2. In large bowl, mix together ground chicken with all seasonings until well incorporated.
3. Divide mixture into 12 equal portions
4. Roll into balls, then flatten into thin patties in heated skillet
5. Cook for 2-3 minutes on each side or until browned and cooked through (may use meat thermometer to make sure cooked to safe poultry temperature)

| Lunch 0 Point Weight Loss Meals

Healthy Lunch Box

Prep Time	**Calories**
10 min	**382 kcal**

Ingredients :

- 4 cups Cooked chicken
- 1 cup Diced peppers
- 1 cup Sliced cucumbers
- 2 Sliced apples
- 2 cups Grapes
- 4 Hard boiled eggs
- Some of my greek yogurt dip!

Instructions :

1. Place all your ingredients in your Lunch boxes containers, seal and refrigerate until ready to use.

2. Use with in 3 days

Per serving: Carbohydrates: 29g (10%)
Protein: 42g (84%)Fat: 14g (22%) Saturated Fat: 4g (20%)
Cholesterol: 291mg (97%) Sodium: 171mg (7%)
Potassium: 735mg (21%)Fiber: 3g (12%) Sugar: 23g (26%)Vitamin
A: 580IU (12%) Vitamin C: 37.6mg (46%)
Calcium: 63mg (6%)Iron: 2.9mg (16%)

| Bistro Box

Prep Time	Cook Time	Calories
10 min	XXXX	99 kcal

| Ingredients :

- 1 packet of Hidden Valley Greek Yogurt Dips Mix
- 1 1/2 cups of plain fat free greek yogurt
- 4 hardboiled eggs
- Chicken breast from rotisserie chicken skin removed
- 1 pint grape tomatoes rinsed and patted dry

- baby carrots rinsed and patted dry
- apples rinsed, patted dry, sliced and lightly brushed with lemon juice
- fresh grapes rinsed and patted dry
- salt and freshly ground pepper

| Instructions :

1. In a small bowl, combine Hidden Valley Greek Yogurts Dips mix and fat free greek yogurt.

2. Fill portion cups with ranch dip, cover with portion cup lids and set aside. You will have leftover ranch dip.

3. Assemble bistro box as pictured.

4. Sprinkle chicken and hardball eggs with a pinch of kosher salt and freshly ground pepper.

5. Keep refrigerated and store up to three days.

Per serving:

Fat 6g9%	Potassium 343mg10%	Protein 7g14%
Saturated Fat 2g13%	Carbohydrates 5g2%	Vitamin A 1245IU25%
Cholesterol 187mg 62%	Fiber 1g4%	Vitamin C 16mg19%
Sodium 68mg3%	Sugar 4g4%	Calcium 37mg4

Chili

Prep Time	Cook Time	Calories
10 min	**25 min**	**291 kcal**

Ingredients :

- 1 lb Ground lean chicken or ground lean turkey
- 2 15 oz cans kidney beans, (drained and rinsed)
- 2 15 oz cans black beans, (drained and rinsed)
- 2 15 oz cans pinto beans, (drained and rinsed)
- 3 10 oz cans Rotel Original Diced Tomatoes & Green Chilies
- 1 15 oz can tomato sauce
- 1/2 T cumin
- 1/2 T oregano
- 1 T chili powder
- 2-3 cloves garlic, (minced)
- 1 onion, diced
- 1 lime, quartered

Instructions :

1. Place the ground lean meat in your pressure cooker or Instant Pot. Use the Sauté or Brown function on your device to cook the meat.

2. Pour all of the other ingredients into the pressure cooker except the lime. Quarter your lime and squeeze the juice into the pot. Throw the rind away.

3. Select the Beans/Chili button or Meat/Stew button. Start your machine.

4. Make sure the pressure valve is closed. It will cook for 20 - 35 minutes depending on the machine you use (mine is 20!).

5. Release the pressure from your cooker and serve.

Per serving:: TOTAL FAT: 2.2g SATURATED FAT: 0.2g CHOLESTEROL: 28mg SODIUM: 1127mg CARBOHYDRATES: 45.3g FIBER: 14.2g SUGAR: 5.8g PROTEIN: 24.3g

Buffalo Chicken Lettuce Wraps

Prep Time	Cook Time	Calories
5 min	4 hours	147.5 kcal

Ingredients :

- **For the chicken:**
- 24 oz 3 boneless skinless chicken breasts
- 1 celery stalk, diced
- 1/2 onion, diced
- 1 clove garlic, minced
- 16 oz fat free low sodium chicken broth
- 1/2 cup cayenne pepper sauce, I used Frank's
- **For the wraps:**
- 6 large lettuce leaves, Bibb or Iceberg
- 1 1/2 cups shredded carrots
- 2 large celery stalks, cut into 2 inch matchsticks

Instructions :

1. Combine chicken, onions, celery stalk, garlic and broth (enough to cover your chicken, use water if the can of broth isn't enough) in the Instant Pot.

2. Cover and cook high pressure 15 minutes. Natural release.

3. Remove the chicken from pot, reserve 1/2 cup broth and discard the rest.

4. Shred the chicken with two forks, return to the pot with the 1/2 cup broth and the hot sauce and saute 2 to 3 minutes.

5. Makes 3 cups chicken.

6. To prepare lettuce cups, place 1/2 cup buffalo chicken in each leaf, top with 1/4 cup shredded carrots, celery and dressing of your choice.

7. Wrap up and start eating!

Per serving: Serving: 1/2 cup + veggies, Calories: 147.5kcal, Carbohydrates: 5.2g, Protein: 25g, Fat: 0.1 g, Sodium: 879mg, Fiber: 1.5g, Sugar: 1.5g

Buffalo Chicken Sandwich (without the bread)

Prep Time	Cook Time	Calories

22

10 min　　　　　　　**8 hours**　　　　　　　**272 kcal**

Ingredients :

- 3 lbs boneless skinless chicken breasts
- 12 oz bottle of Buffalo wing sauce
- 1 oz packet of dry Ranch mix.

Instructions :

1. Pour half of the buffalo sauce in the instant pot then top with chicken breasts.

2. Pour the rest of the sauce on top of the chicken and sprinkle with the ranch mix.

3. Place the lid on the instant pot and lock in place making sure the vent is turned to 'sealing'. Set to manual mode (pressure cook setting) for 15 minutes.

4. Let the pressure release naturally once cooking is complete.

5. This will take 10-15 minutes.

Per serving: Carbohydrates: 3g | Protein: 48g | Fat: 6g | Saturated Fat: 1g | Polyunsaturated Fat: 1g | Monounsaturated Fat: 2g | Trans Fat: 1g | Cholesterol: 145mg | Sodium: 2356mg | Potassium: 839mg | Vitamin A: 68IU | Vitamin C: 3mg | Calcium: 11mg | Iron: 1mg

Crockpot Chicken Tortilla Soup

Prep Time	Cook Time	Calories
10min	**6 hours**	**256 kcal**

Ingredients :

- 1 lb skinless,boneless chicken breasts - (diced)
- 1 red onion - (diced)
- 1 15 oz can white beans - (drained and rinsed)
- 1 15 oz can black beans - (drained and rinsed)
- 1 15 oz can corn - (drained and rinsed)

- 1 4 oz can diced green chiles
- 1 28 oz can diced tomatoes
- 2 cups fat free chicken broth
- 1 tbsp chili powder
- 1 tbsp cumin
- 4 garlic cloves - (minced)
- Salt and pepper to taste.

Instructions :

Combine all ingredients in a slow cooker, and cook on low for 6-8 hours.

Per serving:
Carbohydrates: 31.3 g (10%)Protein: 26 g (52%)Fat: 3.4 g (5%)Saturated
Fat: 0.3 g (2%)Cholesterol: 48 mg (16%)Sodium: 532 mg (23%)Potassium: 841 mg (24%)Fiber: 7.6 g (32%)Sugar: 4.3 g (5%)Calcium: 70 mg (7%)Iron: 4.1 mg (23%)

Notes : The entire recipe makes 6 servings, The serving size is 1 1/2 cups

Greek Chickpea Salad

Calories

192 kcal

Ingredients :

- 2 (15 ounce) cans chickpea, drained and rinsed
- 1 small tomato, chopped
- 1/4 cup finely chopped red onion
- 1/2 teaspoon sugar
- 1/4 cup reduced fat crumbled feta cheese
- 1/2 tablespoon lemon juice
- 1/2 tablespoon red wine vinegar
- 1 tablespoon plain nonfat Greek Yogurt
- 2 cloves garlic, minced
- 1/4 teaspoon salt
- 1/4 teaspoon pepper
- 1-2 tablespoons cilantro

Instructions :

1. Drain and rinse the chickpeas and place in a medium bowl.
2. Toss in the rest of the ingredients until chickpeas are evenly coated and all of the ingredients are mixed well.
3. Serve immediately and refrigerate any leftovers.
4. I ate ours over the coarse of a few days and loved it every time.

Per serving:

Fat 4g 6%

Saturated Fat 1g 6%

Cholesterol 4mg1

Sodium 1297mg 56%

Carbohydrates 32g 11%

Fiber 8g 33%

Sugar 6g 7%

Protein 10g 20%

| Taco Soup

Prep Time	Cook Time	Calories
5 min	4 hours	306 kcal

| Ingredients :

- 1 lb. boneless skinless chicken breast
- 1 onion, diced
- 2 garlic cloves, minced
- 14.5 oz. canned pinto beans, drained
- 14.5 oz. canned black beans, drained
- 14.5 oz. canned corn, drained
- 14.5 oz. canned diced tomatoes with green chilies (not drained)
- 2 cups fat free chicken broth
- 1.25 oz. taco seasoning

| Instructions :

1. **Slow Cooker Option:** Add everything to the slow cooker.
2. Cook on low for 4 hours (up to 8 is fine).
3. Remove the chicken and shred or chop.
4. **Stovetop:** Add a touch of olive to a large soup pot. Cook the onions for 6-8 minutes until tender. Add the garlic and cook for 1 minute until fragrant.
5. Add the remaining ingredients and bring to a simmer. Cover and cook for 30 minutes.
6. To keep the chicken as tender as possible, I like to remove it after 12-15 minutes when it is cooked through.
7. Then I shred or chop it and add it back to the soup before serving.

Per serving:

Total Fat 3g	Sodium 1573mg	Protein 28g
Cholesterol 37mg	Total Carbohydrate 44g	

Instant Pot Chicken Zoodle Soup

Prep Time	Cook Time	Calories
10 min	**35 min**	**103 kcal**

Ingredients :

- 1 lb. raw boneless skinless chicken breasts
- 1/4 tsp. each salt and black pepper
- 6 cups reduced-sodium chicken broth
- 1 cup chopped onion
- 1 cup chopped carrots
- 1/2 cup chopped celery
- 2 tsp. chopped garlic
- 1/2 tsp. onion powder
- 1/2 tsp. ground thyme
- 2 bay leaves
- 10 oz. (about 2 small) zucchini
- Optional seasonings: additional salt and black pepper

Instructions :

1. Place chicken in the Instant Pot, and sprinkle with salt and pepper.

2. Add all remaining ingredients except zucchini.

3. Seal with lid. Manual/Pressure Cook, and set for 8 minutes. (The Instant Pot will preheat for 20 - 25 minutes.)

4. Meanwhile, using a spiral vegetable slicer, cut zucchini into spaghetti-like noodles. (If you don't have a spiral veggie slicer, peel zucchini into super-thin strips, rotating the zucchini after each strip.)

5. Roughly chop for shorter noodles.Press Keep Warm/Cancel. Caution: During the next step, keep hands and face away from opening; the fast-escaping steam will be hot!

6. Vent to release steam.Remove and discard bay leaves. Transfer chicken to a large bowl. Shred with two forks.

7. Add zucchini noodles and shredded chicken to the Instant Pot. Re-cover and let sit for 8 minutes, or until noodles have slightly softened.

Per serving: 1/8th of recipe (about 1 cup): 103 calories, 2g total fat (0.5g sat. fat), 533mg sodium, 6g carbs, 1.5g fiber, 3g sugars, 14.5g protein

Chickpea Tuna Salad

Calories

273 kcal

Ingredients :

- 15 ounce can chickpeas, rinsed and drained
- 6 ounce can wild albacore tuna, drained
- 1 to 2 tablespoons chopped red onion
- 2 tablespoons capers, plus 2 tablespoons of the brine
- 2 tablespoons red wine vinegar
- chopped lettuce, optional

Instructions :

Combine all the ingredients, adjust the vinegar and brine to your taste.

Per serving: 27 Protein 36 Carbs 2.5 Fats

Crockpot Chicken Soup

Ingredients :

- 2 pounds of skinless chicken breasts

- Reduced sodium chicken brother or vegetable broth (or even just plain water)

- 3 to 4 cups of your favorite chopped vegetables (such as carrots, peas, corn, broccoli, and/or celery.

- Salt, pepper, and/or garlic to taste

Instructions :

1. Put all ingredients in crock pot.

2. Cook on low for 7 hours or on high for 4 hours.

3. Enjoy!

Per serving: SmartPoints myWW Green: 1 Pts, myWW Blue: 0 Pts, myWW Purple: 0 Pts

| Shrimp Ceviche

Prep Time	Cook Time
10 min	**10 min**

| Ingredients :

- Cooked shrimp ½ cup(s), chopped
- Fresh tomato(es) ½ small, finely chopped
- Cucumber(s) ½ small, Kirby, finely chopped
- Uncooked red onion(s) 2 Tbsp, chopped

- Fresh lime juice 2 Tbsp
- Cilantro 2 tsp, fresh, chopped
- Table salt 1 pinch(es), or to taste
- Black pepper 1 pinch(es), or to taste

| Instructions :

1. In a medium bowl, combine the shrimp, tomato, cucumber, onions, and lime juice; let stand for 10 minutes for the flavors to blend.

2. Sprinkle with the cilantro; season with salt and black pepper.

Per serving: 1 bowl

Chicken Vegetable Soup

Prep Time	Cook Time	Calories
20 min	**7 hours**	**150 kcal**

Ingredients :

- 1-½ pounds raw boneless skinless lean chicken breasts
- ½ teaspoon salt
- ⅛ teaspoon black pepper
- ½ cup finely diced onion
- 2 carrots, chopped
- 3 cups dry coleslaw mix (shredded cabbage and carrots)

- 2 cans (14 to 15 ounces each) low-sodium chicken broth
- 1 can (14 to 15 ounces) cannellini (white kidney) beans, drained and rinsed
- 1 can (14 to 15 ounces) stewed tomatoes, not drained
- 1 cup frozen peas
- 1 teaspoon dried thyme leaves
- 1 bay leaf

Instructions :

1. Ideal slow cooker size: 6-Quart.

2. Evenly season chicken with ¼ teaspoon salt and the pepper. Place all ingredients in the crock pot and stir.

3. Cover and cook on HIGH for 3 to 4 hours, or on LOW for 6 - 8 hours, until chicken is fully cooked and the vegetables are tender.

4. Remove and discard the bay leaf.

5. Remove the chicken and place in a bowl. Shred each piece using two forks -- one to hold the chicken in place and the other to scrape across the meat and shred it.

6. Return the shredded chicken to the crock pot and stir into the soup.

7. Season to taste with salt and pepper.

Per serving: Fat 1g 2%, Carbohydrates 15g 5%, Fiber 4g 16%, Protein 20g

| Asian Chicken Soup

Calories

169 kcal

| Ingredients :

- 1 pound boneless, skinless chicken breast
- 8 ounces fresh mushrooms
- 2 tablespoons lemon juice
- 1 teaspoon garlic, minced
- 1 teaspoon fresh ginger, ground

- 2 cups fat-free chicken broth
- 2 tablespoons reduced-sodium soy sauce
- 3 scallions, thinly sliced
- 1 leek

| Instructions :

1. Cook the chicken, mushrooms, lemon juice, garlic and ginger in a medium saucepan over medium heat about 5 minutes.

2. You may recognize this next step (the leek) from our Creamy Chicken and Stuffing Casserole. (I hope we can all agree that leeks are cool at this point, and totally worth including in this healthy soup).

3. Meanwhile, cut the top of the leek off (the darkest green part). You will not be using the top half so that part can be discarded.

4. Slice into the bottom portion of the leek going lengthwise starting about 1-2 inches from the bottom of the leek.

5. Rotate the leek and slice it the lengthwise again. Do this a couple of more times until you have very thin sliced strips (still connected to the stem at the bottom at this point).

6. Now chop the leek into small pieces starting from the top.

7. Rinse the small pieces of the leek.

8. Add broth, soy sauce, scallions and leek and cook for 7-8 more minutes.

Per serving: Fat 3g 5%, Cholesterol 68mg 23%, Sodium 490mg 21%, Carbohydrates 3g 1%, Fiber 1g 4%, Protein 22g 44%

Dinner 0 Point Weight Loss Meals

| Crockpot Santa Fe Chicken

Prep Time	**Cook Time**	**Calories**
5 min	**8 hours**	**183 kcal**

| Ingredients :

- 24 oz chicken breast, (1-1/2 lbs)
- 14.4 oz can diced tomatoes with mild green chilies
- 15 oz can black beans, rinsed and drained
- 8 oz frozen corn
- 1/4 cup chopped fresh cilantro
- 14.4 oz can chicken broth
- 3 scallions, chopped
- 1 tsp garlic powder
- 1 tsp onion powder
- 1 tsp cumin
- 1 tsp cayenne pepper, to taste
- salt to taste

| Instructions :

1. Combine chicken broth, beans (drained), corn, tomatoes, cilantro, scallions, garlic powder, onion powder, cumin, cayenne pepper and salt in the slow cooker.

2. Season chicken breast with salt and lay on top.

3. Cook on low for 8 - 10 hours or on high for 4 to 6 hours.

4. Thirty minutes before serving, remove chicken and shred.

5. Return chicken to slow cooker and stir in. Adjust salt and seasoning to taste.

6. Serve over rice or tortillas and with your favorite toppings.

Per serving: Serving: 3/4 cup, Calories: 183kcal, Carbohydrates: 17g, Protein: 24g, Fat: 3g, Saturated Fat: 0.5g, Cholesterol: 62.5mg, Sodium: 557.5mg, Fiber: 3.5g, Sugar: 3.5g WW Points Plus:5

| Chicken Fajitas

Prep Time	Cook Time	Calories
15 min	**10 min**	**217 kcal**

| Ingredients :

- 2 chicken breasts thinly sliced
- 1 red onion thinly sliced
- 1 yellow sweet pepper de-seeded & thinly sliced
- 1 red sweet pepper de-seeded & thinly sliced

- **For the marinade :**
- 1.5 tsp smoked paprika
- 1 tsp ground coriander
- ½ tsp ground cumin
- 1 garlic clove minced
- 4 drops chili sauce optional
- 5 sprays Frylight / Pam

| Instructions :

1. Mix the smoked paprika, ground coriander, ground cumin, minced garlic and chili sauce (if using) in a bowl and add the thinly sliced chicken.Toss the chicken strips in the spice mix until they are thoroughly covered in the spices. Set aside.

2. Finely slice the peppers and onion. Heat a large frying pan over a high heat with 10 sprays of a calorie controlled cooking spray oil (such as Pam or Frylight).

3. Add the chicken strips and cook for 1 - 2 minutes until they start to colour. Add the onions and peppers and keep stirring over a high heat for 5 - 7 minutes until all the ingredients are brown.

4. You want the fajita to have a bit of a charred look but you don't want it to burn. If it starts sticking to the bottom of the pan add a couple of tbsp of water.

5. Check that the chicken is cooked by cutting the biggest bit that you can find in half and checking the inside, if it is still raw then carry on cooking till it is cooked through.

6. If you are using tortillas, place them in the oven for 2 - 3 minutes to warm up before serving.

Per serving: Fat 6 g 9 % , Cholesterol 72 mg 24 %, Sodium 194 mg 8 %, Potassium 815 mg 23 %, Carbohydrates 15 g 5 %, Fiber 4 g 17 %, Sugar 5 g 6 %, Protein 26 g 52 %

| Chicken Egg Roll in a Bowl

| Ingredients :

- 1 tsp minced ginger
- 4 1/2 cup(s) packaged coleslaw mix (shredded cabbage and carrots)
- 1/2 cup(s) shredded carrots
- 3 medium scallions
- 3 Tbsp low sodium soy sauce
- 1 1/2 teaspoon sesame oil
- 1 pound(s) ground chicken breast (98% FF)

| Instructions :

1. Brown your choice of meat in a medium non stick skillet until cooked all the way through and then add the ginger.

2. Add soy sauce and sesame oil.

3. Add full bag of coleslaw, stir till coated with sauce

4. Add ½ cup of shredded carrots, stir till coated with sauce

5. Add chopped scallions, mix thoroughly and cook on medium high heat until the cole slaw has reduced by half.

Serving Size: about 1 ½ cups

Spicy Chicken Chili

Prep Time	Cook Time	Calories
5 min	**20 min**	**80 kcal**

Ingredients :

- 2 cups cooked chicken shredded
- ½ cup chopped onions
- 1 can 15 oz pinto beans
- 1 can 16 oz. kidney beans'1 can diced tomatoes
- 2 cups chicken stock
- ½ cup red salsa
- ½ cup water
- 1 clove minced garlic
- 1 can green chilis
- 1 teaspoon ground cumin
- 1 teaspoon chili powder
- 1 teaspoon salt
- ¼ teaspoon pepper

Instructions :

1. Combine all ingredients in a pot on the stove over medium-high heat.
2. Heat until boiling.
3. Reduce heat and simmer 20 minutes (covered)over medium-low heat.

Per serving:

Carbohydrates:1g	Saturated Fat: 1g	Potassium:121mg
Protein: 12g	Cholesterol:35mg	Fiber: 1g
Fat: 3g	Sodium: 430mg	

Dump-and-Bake Salsa Chicken

Prep Time	Cook Time	Calories
10 min	45 min	324 kcal

Ingredients :

- 1 (14.4 ounce) bag frozen corn kernels (about 3 cups)
- 1 (15 ounce) can black beans, drained and rinsed
- 1 (15 ounce) can petite diced tomatoes, drained
- 1 cup salsa, divided
- 1 teaspoon minced garlic
- ½ teaspoon cumin
- 2 lbs. boneless, skinless chicken breasts
- Salt and pepper, to taste

Instructions :

1. Preheat oven to 375 degrees F.

2. Spray a large (9 x 13-inch) baking dish with cooking spray.

3. In the prepared dish, stir together frozen corn, black beans, diced tomatoes, ½ cup of salsa, garlic, and cumin.

4. Place chicken on top of corn mixture. Season chicken with salt and pepper, to taste.

5. Pour remaining ½ cup of salsa over chicken.

6. Cover tightly with foil and bake for approximately 45-60 minutes, or until internal temperature of chicken reaches 165 degrees F. The total length of cooking time will vary depending on the size of your chicken breasts.

7. Remove chicken from dish and slice (or shred with two forks). Return to dish, stir to combine, and serve.

Per serving: Serving: 1/6 of the recipe, Carbohydrates: 36.7g , Protein: 42g, Fat: 2.9g, Saturated Fat: 0.6g, Cholesterol: 88mg, Sodium: 434mg, Fiber: 7g, Sugar: 7.3g

Instant Pot Chicken Taco Soup

Calories

181.89 kcal

Ingredients :

- 1 small onion chopped
- 1 15.5 oz can seasoned black beans drained
- 1 15.5 oz can light kidney beans drained
- 1 8 oz can tomato sauce
- 10 oz bag frozen corn
- 2 10 oz cans diced tomatoes with green chilis
- 1 packet taco seasoning
- 1 tsp cumin
- 1 tsp chili powder
- 2 boneless skinless chicken breast
- ½ cup water

Instructions :

1. Place all ingredients in your Instant Pot.
2. Make sure seal is in lid properly, apply lid, set vent to sealing.
3. Set instant pot to soup (or you can use manual) with high pressure for 8 minutes.
4. Allow to natural pressure release by not touching the vent for 10 minutes.
5. Shred chicken breast with two forks and place back in pot

Per serving: Carbohydrates: 27.02g | Protein: 16.26g | Fat: 1.71g | Fiber: 7.75g

| Mexican Stir Fry

Prep Time	**Cook Time**
5 min	**4 hours**

| Ingredients :

- 1 lb Boneless chicken cubed
- 14.5 ounces canned black beans, rinsed & drained
- 12 ounces frozen corn
- 1 Onion chopped

- 2 Cloves garlic minced
- 1 tsp Cumin
- Salt to taste
- black pepper to taste
- 2 Limes juiced

| Instructions :

1. Get your slow cooker ready, spray it with nonstick cooking spray.

2. Then combine your chicken, corn, black beans, cumin, garlic, lime juice, and onion to your crockpot.

3. Cook on low for 8 hours or high for 4 hours.

4. During the last 30 minutes of cook time cook 2 cups of rice according to cooking direction on rice package. You can also make baked rice if you want to.

5. Put rice on to your plate, then top with the slow cooker Mexican stir fry, and squeeze a little bit of lime juice on top if you want to add more to your meal.

makes 4 servings

| Crockpot Chicken Verde

| Ingredients :

- 1 Pound Boneless Skinless
- Chicken Breasts
- 6 Tomatillos peeled and quartered
- 2 Jalapenos Seeded
- ½ White Onion quartered
- 2 cloves garlic, minced
- ½ Cup Fat-Free Low Sodium Chicken Broth
- ½-1 teaspoon Cumin (use less if you prefer a milder taste)
- ½ Teaspoon Salt
- ¼ Teaspoon Black Pepper

| Instructions :

1. In blender purée all ingredients except for chicken until a slightly chunky.
2. Place chicken in bottom of crock pot and pour purée over top
3. Cook on low heat for 6 hours
4. Shred chicken and serve with extra sauce over top

Instant Pot Pineapple Chicken

Prep Time	Cook Time
3 min	**12 min**

Ingredients :

- 3 pounds boneless skinless chicken breast
- 1/2 cup homemade pineapple salsa
- 2 cups pineapple chunks (in it's own natural juices)- drained
- 1/4 teaspoon cajun seasoning
- 1 teaspoon sea salt
- 1 1/2 cups water

Instructions :

1. MAKE SURE YOUR POT LINER IS IN YOUR INSTANT POT!

2. Place all ingredients into the pot liner of your Instant Pot.

3. Close and lock the lid, and turn the vent to closed position.

4. Place on High Manual Pressure for 12 minutes, and allow to NPR.

5. Once depressurized, open the vent to ensure that all pressure has been released.

6. Pull out the chicken breasts onto a plate or cutting board, and shred with forks. Once the chicken is shredded, add it back into your IP. Let it set for a couple of minutes to marinate in that pineapple yumminess!

Chipotle Chicken Casserole

Prep Time	Cook Time	Calories
10 min	40 min	382 kcal

Ingredients :

- 4 medium chicken breasts skinless and without bones
- 2 can tinned chopped tomatoes 2 x 400g (14.5oz) can
- 1 tbsp cajun seasoning (7g)
- 1.5 tsp chipotle paste more if you like spicy!
- .5 tbsp ground cumin
- 1 can black beans 1 x 400g (14.5oz) can - drained & rinsed
- 1 can haricot / pinto / cannellini 1 x 400g (14.5oz) can - drained & rinsed
- 1 can sweetcorn 1 x 400g (14.5oz) can - drained
- 4 tbsp fat free Greek yogurt optional

Instructions :

1. Preheat the oven to 200oC / 180oC / Gas Mark 6 / 400oF

2. Place the chicken breasts in the bottom of a large, deep casserole dish. Top with the beans, tomatoes, corn, chipotle paste, ground cumin and Cajun seasoning. Stir to combine.

3. Cover the casserole with kitchen foil (or casserole lid if you have one). Bake in the oven for 20 minutes.

4. After 20 minutes, remove from the oven and remove the kitchen foil / casserole lid. Stir and place back in the oven, uncovered for a further 15 - 20 minutes or until the chicken is cooked through.

5. Top with a tablespoon of 0% Fat Free Greek yogurt (optional).

Slow Cooker Chicken Cacciatore

Prep Time	Cook Time	Calories
30 min	4 hours	311 kcal

Ingredients :

- Uncooked boneless skinless chicken thigh(s) 1 pound(s), boneless, cut into bite-size pieces
- Fresh mushroom(s) 1 cup(s), sliced (fresh, frozen or canned)
- Green pepper(s) 1 strip(s), sliced (fresh or frozen)
- Uncooked onion(s) 1 cup(s), chopped (fresh or frozen)
- Garlic clove(s) 1 clove(s), large, minced
- Canned tomato paste 1 tbsp(s)
- Canned crushed tomatoes 14½ oz, fire-roasted
- Red wine ¼ fl oz, dry-variety
- Dried oregano ¾ tsp(s), crushed
- Table salt ¾ tsp(s), divided
- Black pepper ¼ pinch

Instructions :

1. Place chicken in a 3- to 5-quart slow cooker.

2. Add mushrooms, green pepper, onion, garlic, tomato paste, tomatoes and juice, wine, oregano, 1/2 teaspoon of salt and black pepper.

3. Cover slow cooker; cook on high heat for 5 to 6 hours or on low heat for 6 to 8 hours.

4. Taste just before serving and add remaining 1/4 teaspoon of salt if necessary.

5. Yields about 1 cup per serving.

Baked Chicken Fajita Soup

Prep Time	Cook Time	Calories
5 min	**35 min**	**226 kcal**

Ingredients :

- 1 pound boneless skinless chicken breasts, cut into strips
- 1 medium onion, sliced
- 1 bell pepper, sliced
- 1 ripe tomato, cubed
- 1 tablespoon cumin
- 2 teaspoons garlic powder
- 1 teaspoon onion powder
- 1 teaspoon salt
- 1 teaspoon black pepper
- ½ teaspoon chili powder (more or less to taste)

Instructions :

1. Preheat oven to 375 degrees
2. Spray medium casserole dish with non-stick spray
3. Mix together seasonings in small bowl
4. Cut chicken into bite sized pieces or strips and coat well with seasoning blend
5. Place in single layer in bottom of casserole dish
6. Top with vegetables
7. Bake at 375 degrees for 35-40 minutes or until vegetables have browned and chicken is cooked through.

Per serving: FAT: 5g, SATURATED FAT: 1g, TRANS FAT: 0g, UNSATURATED FAT: 3g, CHOLESTEROL: 96mg, SODIUM: 629mg, CARBOHYDRATES: 8g, FIBER: 2g, SUGAR: 3g, PROTEIN: 37g

Persian Chicken Kabobs

Prep Time	Cook Time	Calories
4 hours and 10min	**15 min**	**202 kcal**

Ingredients :

- 1.33 lbs. boneless skinless chicken breast, cut into 1 inch chunks
- 1 cup nonfat plain yogurt
- 1/2 cup parsley
- 4 garlic cloves, minced
- 1 lemon, juice and zest
- 1 tsp. cumin
- 1 tsp. onion powder
- 1 tsp. black pepper
- 1 tsp. salt
- 1/2 tsp. paprika
- 1/2 tsp. coriander

Instructions :

1. Combine the yogurt, parsley, garlic, lemon juice, lemon zest, cumin, onion powder, black pepper, salt, paprika, and coriander.

2. Marinate the chicken in this mixture for at least 4 hours or overnight.

3. When ready to cook, remove the chicken from the marinade, letting excess drip off.

4. Thread onto skewers. These can also be cooked without the skewers. If making skewers,consider adding some of your favorite veggies.

5. To grill: Place on a medium hot grill for 10-15 minutes, turning 2-3 times, or until chicken is fully cooked.

6. To broil: Place on a foil lined baking sheet. Broil for 10-12 minutes, turning 1-2 times, or until chicken is cooked through.

Per serving: 9g CARBS1g FAT36g PROTEIN

Slow Cooker Mexican Shredded Chicken

Prep Time	Cook Time	Calories
10 min	**8 hours**	**67 kcal**

Ingredients :

- 2 lbs boneless skinless chicken breast, raw
- 1 medium yellow onion chopped
- 3 cloves garlic
- 2 tsp vegetable oil (or olive oil)
- 1 15 oz can tomato sauce
- 1 4 oz can diced green chiles
- 1 cup chicken broth 98% fat free
- 1 tbs cumin
- 1 tbs chili powder
- 2 tsp coriander (in the spice aisle)
- 1 1/2 tsp kosher salt
- 1 tsp pepper
- a few dashes of your favorite hot sauce

Instructions :

1. In a medium skillet heat oil and add onions and garlic. Cook until soft or about 5 minutes and then add to slow cooker.

2. Add the rest of ingredients to slow cooker and mix until combined well.

3. Cook on low for 7-8 hour on low or high for 5 hours.. Remove chicken from sauce, shred, and return to slow cooker for 20-30 minutes to allow the flavors from the sauce to mingle with the chicken.

4. Enjoy chicken with tacos, salads, enchiladas, burrito bowls, quesadillas, or whatever ya want!

Serving size: 1/2 cup (3.5 oz) / 9g fat, .2g saturated fat, 2.3g carbohydrates, .5g fiber, .7g sugar, 11g protein.

Slow Cooker Tex Mex Chicken and Beans

Prep Time	Cook Time	Calories
15min	**8 hours**	**440 kcal**

Ingredients :

- 1 cup dried pinto beans, rinsed and soaked in water for at least a couple of hours
- One 16 ounce jar mild or medium salsa
- 2 tablespoons chopped canned chipotle in adobo sauce
- 2 tablespoons all purpose flour
- 1 medium red onion, chopped
- 1 medium red bell pepper, seeds and ribs removed, chopped
- coarse salt and freshly ground black pepper
- 1½ pounds boneless, skinless chicken
- ¼ cup chopped fresh cilantro, for serving

Instructions :

1. In a 5 to 6 quart slow cooker, stir together drained beans, salsa, chiles, flour, 1 cup water, onion and bell pepper.

2. Cover and cook on low heat for 4 hours. Season chicken generously with salt and pepper; arrange on top of bean mixture, add another cup of water, and cook on low heat for 4 more hours.

3. Shred chicken, and stir.

4. Serve over brown rice, or inside flour tortillas to make tacos (not included in the nutritional).

5. Garnish with cilantro and additional desired toppings.

Per serving: Carbohydrates: 46g, Protein: 46g, Fat: 8g, Saturated Fat: 2g, Polyunsaturated Fat: 2g, Monounsaturated Fat: 3g, Trans Fat: 0.03g, Cholesterol: 162mg, Sodium: 1290mg, Potassium: 1494mg, Fiber: 11g, Sugar: 8g, Vitamin A: 1960IU, Vitamin C: 46mg, Calcium: 111mg, Iron: 5mg

AIR FRYER CHICKEN BREAST

Prep Time	Cook Time	Calories
5min	10 min	208 kcal

Ingredients :

- kosher salt
- 4 boneless chicken breasts, about 6 ounces each
- olive oil spray
- 3/4 teaspoon garlic powder
- 3/4 teaspoon onion powder
- 1/2 teaspoon dried parsley
- 1/2 teaspoon smoked paprika
- 1/8 cayenne pepper

Instructions :

1. Pound the thicker end of the chicken to make both sides leveled out so they cook evenly.

2. Fill a large bowl with 6 cups of lukewarm water and add 1/4 cup Diamond Crystal kosher salt, stir to dissolve.

3. Add the chicken breasts to the water and let them sit, refrigerated 1 to 1 1/2 hours to brine. Remove from water, pat dry with paper towels and discard the water.

4. In a small bowl combine 3/4 teaspoon salt, with the remaining spices. Spritz the chicken with oil and rub all over, then rub the spice mix over the chicken.

5. Add the chicken to the air fryer basket and air fry in batches 380F 5 minutes on each side, 10 minutes total until browned on the outside and cooked through on the inside. See notes below for larger breasts.

Serving: 1breast, Calories: 208kcal, Carbohydrates: 1g, Protein: 39g, Fat: 4.5g, Saturated
Fat: 1g, Cholesterol: 124.5mg, Sodium: 77mg, Fiber: 0.5g, Sugar: 0.5g

WW Points Plus:5

Baked Chicken with Lemon & Fresh Herbs

Prep Time	Cook Time
10 min	**35min**

Ingredients :

- Cooking spray 4 spray(s)
- Uncooked boneless skinless chicken breast(s) 1 pound(s), four 4 oz halves
- Table salt ½ tsp
- Black pepper ¼ tsp, freshly ground
- Olive oil 1 tsp

- Fresh lemon juice 2 tsp, or more to taste
- Rosemary 2 tsp, fresh, chopped
- Fresh parsley 2 tsp, chopped
- Reduced-sodium chicken broth ¼ cup(s)
- Lemon(s) ½ medium, quartered (for garnish)

Instructions :

1. Preheat oven to 400°F. Coat a small, shallow roasting pan with cooking spray.

2. Season both sides of chicken with salt and pepper.

3. Transfer chicken to prepared pan and drizzle with oil; sprinkle with lemon juice, rosemary and parsley.

4. Pour broth around chicken to coat bottom of pan.

5. Bake until chicken is cooked through, about 30 to 35 minutes. Garnish with fresh lemon and serve.

Serving size: 1 chicken breast half

Pepperoncini Chicken

Prep Time	Cook Time	Calories
5min	**4 hours**	**208 kcal**

Ingredients :

- lbs boneless skinless chicken breast
- 1 cup low sodium chicken broth
- 8 oz. pepperoncinis with liquid
- 2 tbsp. Italian seasoning

Instructions :

1. Add everything to the slow cooker. Cook on low for 4 hours. Shred or slice.

2. Shred or slice the chicken. Taste the chicken and season if needed.

Per serving:

Total Fat 2g

Cholesterol 74mg

Sodium 452mg

Total Carbohydrate 2g

Protein 33g

Chicken White Bean Salsa Soup

Prep Time	Cook Time	Calories
10 min	**20 min**	**159kcal**

Ingredients :

- 4 cups chicken broth
- 12 ounces salsa (I used red, but green would be good too)
- 2 cans (about 15 ounces each) white beans, drained and rinsed
- 2 cups chopped cooked lean chicken
- 1 to 2 teaspoons chili powder, or to taste
- 1 teaspoon cumin, optional
- Garnish with cilantro, cheese, corn chips, etc., if desired.

Instructions :

1. Empty the salsa into a large saucepan. Cook for 2 minutes over medium-high heat, then add the chicken, beans, broth, chili powder and cumin (if desired).

2. Bring to a boil, lower heat to a simmer, and cook for 10 minutes, stirring occasionally.

3. Alternatively, to make in a slow cooker, add all ingredient into your slow cooker and cook covered on low until hot, about 4 to 6 hours.

4. Use a masher or immersion blender to mash up some of the soup and make it a little thicker if desired.

5. Top each bowl with a sprinkling of green onions or cilantro, a dollop of sour cream, and or some low-fat baked tortilla chips (if desired).

6. Makes about 8 cups of soup.

Per serving: Fat 2.5g

Carbohydrates 15.9g

Fiber 4.4g

Protein 17.7g

Serving size : 1 cup without garnishes

Slow Cooker Tomato Balsamic Chicken

Prep Time	Cook Time	Calories
10 min	**4 hours**	**227 kcal**

Ingredients :

- 2 lbs. boneless and skinless chicken breast
- 28 oz. canned diced tomatoes, half of liquid drained
- 1 sweet onion, sliced thin
- 4 garlic cloves, minced
- 3 tbsp. balsamic vinegar (plus more for serving)
- 1 tbsp. Italian seasoning
- 6 cups fresh spinach
- Salt and pepper.

Instructions :

1. Add the chicken to the slow cooker. Season with salt and pepper.
2. Stir in the remaining ingredients except the spinach.
3. Cook on low for 4 hours adding the spinach during the last 30 minutes of cooking.
4. Taste and season as needed.

   Per serving: 12g CARBS, 2g FAT, 35g PROTEIN

   Notes : Optional: Add fresh mushrooms, spinach, or kale

Ground Turkey Dinner Recipes

| Arizona Burrito Bowls

| Ingredients :

- 16 oz 99% Fat Free Ground Turkey
- 1 packet Taco Seasoning
- 12 oz Riced Cauliflower I used Green Giant brand
- 1/2 bunch Cilantro
- 1 Lime
- 1 can Black Beans, drained
- 1 can Corn, drained
- 1 cup Plain Fat Free Greek Yogurt
- 1 cups Salsa

| Instructions :

1. Cook ground turkey over medium heat in a shallow pan. Add taco seasoning while it's cooking.

2. Microwave riced cauliflower and place in a bowl.

3. Finely chop the cilantro and add to the cauliflower. Zest and juice the lime and add to the cauliflower.

4. Add salt and pepper to taste and stir.. Give it a taste and add more salt as needed.

5. Drain and heat the black beans and corn, either in the microwave or on the stove. Personal choice...

6. Place the rice, turkey, beans and corn in a bowl.

7. Add salsa and yogurt.

serving: 4

| Turkey, Corn and Black Bean Chili

Prep Time	Cook Time	Calories
5min	**8min**	**245 kcal**

| Ingredients :

- 1 pound of ground turkey (99% fat-free)
- 1 15 oz can of black beans, drained
- 1 15 oz can of corn, drained
- ¼ cup water
- 1 tablespoon chili powder
- ½ teaspoon salt
- ¼ teaspoon freshly ground black pepper
- 1 28 ounce can low sodium diced tomatoes (I used crushed)
- 2 chipotle chiles, canned in adobo sauce, chopped
- ¼ cup of fat free cheddar (optional)

| Instructions :

1. Heat a dutch oven over medium-high heat. Coat pan with cooking spray.

2. Add turkey; cook 8 minutes or until browned, stirring to crumble.

3. Stir in corn and black beans; cook 2 minutes.

4. Stir in ¼ cup water and next 5 ingredients stirring until thick. ladle chili into bowls; top with ciilantro and green onions if desired.

   Per serving: Sugar: 4.24, Sodium: 489, Fat: 10.55, Saturated Fat: 2.59, Carbohydrates: 14.09, Fiber: 4, Protein: 23.56

   Notes : Serves 6. Serving Size: 1 cup

Turkey Vegetable Soup

Prep Time	Cook Time	Calories
20 min	**20 min**	**242 kcal**

Ingredients :

- 1 cup finely chopped celery (about 2 stalks)
- ½ cup finely chopped onion
- 1½ teaspoons minced garlic
- 1½ pounds 99% fat free ground turkey breast
- 6 cups fat free beef or chicken broth
- 1 cup sliced carrot (about 2 large)
- ½ cup trimmed fresh green beans, cut into 1-inch lengths
- ½ cup frozen whole kernel corn
- 1½ teaspoons ground cumin
- 1 teaspoon chili powder
- 2 whole bay leaves
- One 15-ounce can kidney beans, rinsed and drained
- One 14.5-ounce can diced tomatoes and green chiles, undrained
- 6 tablespoons shredded Monterey Jack cheese (optional)

Instructions :

1. Heat a Dutch oven over medium-high heat. Coat the pot with nonstick spray.

2. Add the celery, onion, garlic and turkey. Cook for 5 minutes or until the ground turkey is browned, stirring to crumble.

3. Add the chicken/beef broth and remaining ingredients (except cheese); bring to a boil.

4. Cover, reduce heat, and simmer 20 minutes or until the vegetables are tender. Discard the bay leaves.

5. Ladle 2 cups soup into each of 6 bowls; top each serving with 1 tablespoon of cheese (if desired)

Serving: 1serving (2 cups), Calories: 242kcal, Carbohydrates: 22g, Protein: 33g, Fat: 3g, Saturated Fat: 1g, Cholesterol: 62mg, Sodium: 1210mg, Potassium: 910mg, Fiber: 6g, Sugar: 6g, Vitamin A: 3964IU, Vitamin C: 12mg, Calcium: 82mg, Iron: 4mg

3 Bean Turkey Chili

Prep Time	Cook Time	Calories
10 min	**25min**	**231 kcal**

Ingredients :

- 1.3 lb 20 oz 99% lean ground turkey breast
- 1 small onion, chopped
- 1 28 oz can diced tomatoes, drained
- 1 16 oz can tomato sauce
- 1 4.5 oz can chopped chilies
- 1 15 oz can chickpeas, drained
- 1 15.5 oz can black beans, drained
- 1 15.5 oz can small red beans, drained
- 2 tbsp chili powder
- 1 tsp cumin
- **For the Topping:**
- 1/2 cup chopped red onion
- 1/2 cup chopped fresh cilantro for topping
- optional toppings, shredded cheddar, avocado, sour cream, etc

Instructions :

1. Brown turkey and onion in a medium skillet over medium-high heat until cooked through.

2. Transfer to the slow cooker with the beans, chilies, chickpeas, tomatoes, tomato sauce, chili powder and cumin, mixing well.

3. Cook on high 6 to 8 hours or low 10 to 12.

4. Garnish with onions, cilantro and your favorite toppings.

Per serving: 1cup, Calories: 231kcal, Carbohydrates: 27.5g, Protein: 19.5g, Fat: 5g, Saturated Fat: 1.5g, Cholesterol: 42mg, Sodium: 526mg, Fiber: 8g, Sugar: 6.5g WW Points Plus:6

Taco Bowls with Cauliflower Rice

Prep Time	Cook Time	Calories
10 min	**20 min**	**243 kcal**

Ingredients :

- 1/4 cup cilantro
- 1 lime, juice and zest
- 1.33 lb. 99% lean ground turkey (or beef or chicken)
- 3 tbsp taco seasoning
- 2 bell peppers, sliced
- 1 red onion, sliced
- Salt and pepper
- Cooking spray

Instructions :

1. Toss the cauliflower rice with cilantro, lime juice, lime zest, salt, and pepper. Set aside.

2. Heat a skillet over medium-high heat. Add the ground turkey. Cook for 5-7 minutes, breaking it up as you go until the turkey is cooked through.

3. Add half the taco seasoning and cook for 1-2 more minutes to combine. Remove and set aside.

4. Add olive oil to the skillet. Add the peppers and onions. Sprinkle with the remaining taco seasoning.

5. Cook for 5-7 minutes, adding a few tablespoons of water if needed to prevent burning. Stop cooking when the veggies are tender-crisp or cooked to your liking.

6. Assemble the taco bowls by layering the meat and veggies on top of the cilantro lime cauliflower rice.

7. Top with extra cilantro, cheese, salsa or pico de gallo, avocado, or veggies.

8. You can also add black beans, pinto beans, or corn.

Per serving: 14g CARBS, 4g FAT, 39g PROTEIN

| Turkey Pumpkin Chili

Prep Time	**Cook Time**	**Calories**
20 min	**1 hours**	**250 kcal**

| Ingredients :

- 1 pound 99% lean ground turkey
- ¾ cup chopped onions
- ½ cup chopped green bell peppers
- 2 medium garlic cloves, minced
- Two 14.5-ounce cans diced tomatoes, with liquid
- One 15-ounce can unsweetened pure pumpkin puree
- One 15-ounce can kidney beans, with liquid
- One 15-ounce can Great Northern beans, with liquid
- One 15-ounce can tomato sauce
- One 4-ounce can diced green chiles
- 2 teaspoons chili powder
- 1½ teaspoons ground cumin (or more, to taste)
- 1 teaspoon salt
- ½ teaspoon freshly ground black pepper
- 1½ teaspoons oregano
- ½ cup water

| Instructions :

1. In a large pot, add the ground turkey and heat over medium-high until browned.

2. Remove the cooked meat from the pot and place on paper towels to remove any excess fat. Wipe any remaining fat from the pot and coat pot with cooking spray.

3. Sauté onion, bell pepper and garlic; sauté until tender. Return the turkey to the pot.

4. Add all remaining ingredients and stir to combine.

5. Simmer 30 minutes to 1 hour. If the chili is too thick for you, add more water, and adjust seasonings as needed.

Per serving: Carbohydrates: 37g, Protein: 24g, Fat: 2g

Turkey Chili Taco Soup

Prep Time	Cook Time	Calories
5min	15min	225 kcal

Ingredients :

- cooking spray
- 1.3 lbs 99% lean ground turkey
- 1 medium onion, chopped
- 1 bell pepper, chopped
- 10 oz can rotel tomatoes with green chilies
- 15 oz canned or frozen corn, drained
- 15 oz no salt added kidney beans, drained
- 8 oz tomato sauce
- 16 oz fat free refried beans
- 1 packet low-sodium taco seasoning, or use homemade
- 2 1/2 cups less-sodium chicken broth

Instructions :

1. Spray a large pot with cooking spray then brown the turkey over medium heat, breaking up with a wooden spoon as it cooks.

2. When cooked through, add the onions and pepper and cook 2-3 minutes.

3. Add tomatoes, corn, beans, tomato sauce, re-fried beans, taco seasoning and chicken broth.

4. Bring to a boil, cover and simmer about 10-15 minutes.

5. Serve with your favorite toppings such as low fat sour cream, jalapeños, reduced fat cheese, chopped scallions, onions, or chopped fresh cilantro. Freeze leftovers in individual portions for future meals.

Per serving: 22 Protein, 31.5 Carbs, 2 Fats

Side Dish 0 Point Weight Loss Meals

Cucumber Salad

Ingredients :

- In a large measuring cup mix:
- 1/4 c. white vinegar
- 1 TBS lemon juice

- 2 tsp. liquid sweetener (Agave In The Raw)
- 1 tsp. salt
- 1/8 tsp. pepper
- 1/2 tsp. celery seed

Instructions :

1. Stir together and pour over sliced cucumber and onion.
2. In a med/large mixing bowl slice cucumber and onion:
3. 1/2 of a medium sweet onion, sliced (I cut the slices in half and separated the rings)
4. 3-4 medium cucumbers sliced (I used organic).

| Twice Baked Cauliflower

| Ingredients :

- 1 large head of cauliflower, broken into pieces

- ¼ cup of low fat sour cream

- ½ cup cheddar cheese, fat free, shredded

- A dash of olive oil

- Salt, pepper, and garlic powder to taste

| Instructions :

1. Preheat oven to 400 degrees

2. Rinse cauliflower and rip or cut into smaller pieces

3. Place in a large sauce pan and put approximately ¾ cup of water

4. Cover with lid and steam over low flame for about 12 minutes

5. Mash cauliflower with a potato masher

6. Add in sour cream, cheese, and seasonings

7. Add just enough olive oil to a Pyrex dish to coat it

8. Add the cauliflower mixture to the Pyrex dish

9. Bake for about 45 minutes or until crispy on top

| Applesauce

Prep Time	Cook Time	Calories
15min	8hours	83 kcal

| Ingredients :

- 8 medium-large apples, peeled, cored and cut into wedges
- 1/4 cup water
- Cinnamon, to taste

| Instructions :

1. Place the peeled apple wedges into your slow cooker and add water.

2. Cover and cook on low for 8 hours.

3. Mash apples lightly with the back of a spook or a fork (apples will fall apart easily).

4. Add cinnamon (I would start with ½ teaspoon and see if you want more), stir in and continue to cook on low for another 15 minutes.

5. For chunkier applesauce, serve as is.

6. For smooth applesauce, use an immersion blender or place applesauce in a food processor and pulse until desired consistency is reached.

7. Can serve warm or cold. Makes about 3 cups.

Yield: 6 (1/2 CUP) SERVINGS

Nutrition Information : 22 g carbs, 17 g sugars, 0 g fat, 0 g saturated fat, 1 g protein, 2 g fiber

| Roasted Asparagus

Prep Time	Cook Time	Calories
5min	10min	26 kcal

| Ingredients :

- 1 bunch fresh asparagus, about 18 ounces
- olive oil spray
- kosher salt, to taste
- fresh black pepper

| Instructions :

1. Preheat oven to 400°F.

2. Wash and trim hard ends off asparagus. Place in a single layer in roasting pan.

3. Spray all over with olive oil and season with salt and pepper.

4. Roast in oven approximately 10 minutes, or until tender crisp.

Per serving: Serving: 4ounces, Calories: 26kcal, Carbohydrates: 5g, Protein: 2.5g, Sodium: 2mg, Fiber: 2.5g, Sugar: 2g

YIELD:4 SERVINGS

| Slow Cooker Butternut Squash

Ingredients :

- 1 large butternut squash

Instructions :

1. Scrub butternut squash and place in a 6 quart oval slow cooker.

2. Cook on low for 8 hours.

3. After squash is tender, scoop out seeds with spoon and squash from peel.

   Per serving: One cup is 63 calories, 0.1g fat, 0.0g saturated fat, 16.0g carbohydrates, 3.1g sugar, 1.4g protein, 2.8g fiber, 6mg sodium, 0 Freestyle SmartPts

| TROPICAL FRUIT SALAD

Prep Time

Calories

15min

116 kcal

| Ingredients :

- 1 papaya, peeled and diced 3/4-inch cubes (5 cups)
- 2 mangoes, peeled and diced 3/4-inch cubes (2 1/2 cups)
- 1 fresh pineapple, peeled and diced reserving the juice 3/4-inch cubes (4 cups)
- 2 large bananas, peeled and diced 3/4-inch cubes (2 cups)
- 1/4 cup fresh grated coconut, for garnish

| Instructions :

1. Combine the papaya, mangoes, and pineapple in a large bowl and add the juice from the pineapple.

2. Cover and refrigerate until chilled.

3. Just before serving, add the bananas and garnish with fresh coconut.

Per serving: Serving: 11/3 cups, Calories: 116kcal, Carbohydrates: 28g, Protein: 1g, Fat: 1g, Saturated Fat: 0.5g, Sodium: 4mg, Fiber: 3.5g, Sugar: 20g WW Points Plus:0

Quick Chipotle Pinto Beans

Prep Time	Cook Time	Calories
2 min	**13 min**	**110kcal**

Ingredients :

- 2 15 ounce cans pinto beans partially drained
- 1 4 oz can mild green chiles or 1 can Rotel (green chiles & tomatoes)
- 1 chipotle pepper
- 3 tsp adobo sauce
- 1 bay leaf
- 1 tsp kosher salt
- 1 tsp cumin
- 1 tsp garlic powder
- 1 tsp onion powder
- olive oil cooking spray

Instructions :

1. In a medium sauce pan spray bottom with olive oil cooking spray.
2. Add all ingredients to the pan.
3. Stir until combined well.
4. Bring to boil then reduce to medium low heat, cover, and continue to cook for 10-12 minutes until heated through.
5. When heated remove bay leaf and whole chipotle pepper.
6. Serve warm.

Per serving: Makes about 3.5 cups serving size: 1/2 cup WW Green: 3 Points | WW Blue: 0 Points (any amount) | WW Purple: 0 Points (any amount) | 110 calories 1g fat, 0g saturated fat, 19g carbohydrates, 6g fiber, 1g sugar 6g protein

Tomato and Bean Casserole

Prep Time	Cook Time	Calories
XXXX	XXXX	192 kcal

Ingredients :

- 8 cloves garlic, peeled
- 1.5 pounds cherry tomatoes, washed

- 6 springs fresh thyme
- 2 – 15 ounce cans of lima, butter, or white beans, rinsed

Instructions :

1. Heat oven to 400 F.
2. Place garlic, tomatoes, and thyme in a 9x13 casserole dish and bake for 20 minutes until the tomatoes have burst.
3. Add rinsed beans and heat for 10 minutes.
4. Sprinkle the dish with salt and pepper to taste.

Per serving: 192 calories, 0.7 g fat, 0.1 g saturated fat, 35.7 g carbohydrates, 3.4 g sugar, 12.9 g protein, 9 g fiber, 300 mg sodium, 0 Freestyle SmartPts

| Baked Zucchini Chips

| Ingredients :

- 1 zucchini
- canola cooking spray

- seasoned salt, or other seasoning(s) of your choice

| Instructions :

1. Preheat oven to 225 degrees Fahrenheit. Line a baking sheet with parchment paper or nonstick foil, and spray with canola oil. Set aside.

2. Slice zucchini into thin medallions, about the thickness of a quarter. (You can either use a knife & a very steady hand, or a mandoline slicer.)

3. Lay out slices on prepared baking sheet, and spray tops lightly with additional cooking spray. Sprinkle with seasonings of your choice. (A note on seasoning, however - use LESS than what seems appropriate. These shrink considerably in the oven, and if you use too much it gets very concentrated. It's better to end up underseasoning and add more later.)

4. Place in preheated oven and bake 45 minutes. Rotate baking sheet, and bake an additional 30-50 minutes, until chips are browned and crisped to your liking.

5. These are best eaten within a couple hours of removing from the oven, as they start to get chewy if left out. One zucchini makes one serving (1/4 C. - 1/3 C. of chips depending on the size of your squash).

Appetizer & Snack 0 Point Weight Loss Meals

| Red pepper Hummus

Prep Time	**Calories**
3min	**174 kcal**

| Ingredients :

- 1 tin butter beans
- 2 pieces red pepper from a jar (in brine not oil)
- 2 cloves garlic
- 1 tsp smoked paprika
- 1 lemon juice only
- sea salt

| Instructions :

1. Place all the ingredients into your blender/food processor and pulse until it reaches your desired consistency.

2. If the mix seems a bit dry you can add a little water or some of the liquid from the pepper jar.

3. You might want to add more seasoning depending on how you like it!

Per serving: CALORIES 174, CARBS 33G, PROTEIN 8 G, FAT 2 G, SATURATES 0.03 G, SUGARS 2G

| Buffalo Chicken Dip

Prep Time	Cook Time	Calories
5min	4hours	92 kcal

| Ingredients :

- 4 (4oz.) skinless, boneless chicken breast
- 1/2 cup Frank's Buffalo wing sauce

- 1/2 (1 oz.) package or .5 oz dry Hidden Valley Original Ranch Salad Dressing & Seasoning Mix
- 1/2 cup non fat plain or Greek yogurt

| Instructions :

1. Combine first three ingredients into slow cooker for 4-6 hours on low.

2. Using a fork shred chicken and stir in non fat Greek or plain yogurt 30 minutes before serving. Cook on low for an additional 30 minutes

3. Garnish with more buffalo sauce and sliced green onions, if desired.

4. Serve with celery, carrot sticks, prezels, or low point crackers. This dip is also great inside a tortilla or roll for a Buffalo Chicken Wrap or Sandwich.

Per serving: Makes 6 (1/3 cup) servings / TOTAL FAT: 2gSATURATED FAT: 1gTRANS FAT: 0gUNSATURATED FAT: 0gCHOLESTEROL: 42mgSODIUM: 273mgCARBOHYDRATES: 2gFIBER: 0gSUGAR: 1gPROTEIN: 15g

Notes : This dip is great with celery sticks, carrots, thin pretzels, blue cheese crumbles, crackers, or inside a tortilla for wraps, or on a roll for a Buffalo Chicken Sandwich. There are endless possibilities for this dip!

DEVILLED EGGS

Prep Time	**Calories**
30min	**72 kcal**

Ingredients :

- 6 eggs
- 2 tbsp fat free mayonnaise
- 1 - 2 tsp mustard powder or yellow mustard
- ¼ tsp sea salt
- paprika for garnish
- chives chopped for garnish

Instructions :

1. Place the eggs in a saucepan and cover with water. Bring the water to the boil. Once it reaches a boil, reduce the heat so that the water is simmering and set a timer for 7 minutes.

2. Once the timer goes off, remove the saucepan from the heat and drain off the hot water. Run the eggs under cold running water for a couple of minutes until they are cold enough to handle.

3. Peel the eggs (see tips in post) and slice each egg length-ways.

4. Remove the yolks and place them in a small bowl with the mayonnaise, mustard powder and salt. Mix till you have a smooth creamy consistency. Taste and add more mustard or salt if required.

5. Either spoon the yolk mixture into the egg whites, or fill a piping bag fitted with a large star nozzle and pipe the mixture onto the egg whites.

6. Sprinkle with a pinch of paprika and some chopped chives.

Per serving: Fat 5g, Carbohydrates 1g, Protein 6g

Crock Pot Marinara Sauce

Prep Time	Cook Time
5min	**8 hours**

Ingredients :

- 3 cans 28 oz crushed tomatoes
- 2 14.5 oz cans fire roasted diced tomatoes drained
- 8 garlic cloves minced
- 1 yellow large onion diced
- 2 tbsp dried oregano

- 2 tbsp dried basil
- 1/4 tsp red pepper flakes more or less depending on the level of spice you'd like
- 1-½ tsp kosher salt
- 1 teaspoon pepper
- 1-2 bay leaves (optional)

Instructions :

1. Stir all of your ingredients in a 6 quart slow cooker. Cook on low for 8-10 hours to really get all of those lovely flavors to mingle and fall in love with each other.

   Salt and Pepper to taste when finished.

2. **For smoother sauce:** use an immersion hand blender, or put in a blender. Blend on low until desired consistency.

   For thicker sauce: tilt the lid off of the crockpot and cook on high for about 30-60 minutes. This will reduce the sauce some so that it's thicker. Depending on the canned tomatoes sometimes the sauce can be a bit more "water-y".

   Reheating after freezing: You can add sauce to your favorite recipe. If you think it seems a bit "water-y" this is normal and can happen depending on the actual tomatoes after they were picked and canned. You can put sauce in a pot on the stove without a cover and heat over medium-low heat reducing it until you reach desired consistency.

3. **Freezing instructions:** Let cool completely. I usually add about 2 cups to each freezer bag, press as much air out as possible, close the bag, and then stack on top of eachother in the freezer to save space.

Brownie Batter Chocolate Hummus

Prep Time	Calories
7min	**80kcal**

Ingredients :

- 14 oz. canned chickpeas, drained and rinsed
- 1/4 cup cocoa powder
- 2 tsp. Stevia (or maple syrup)
- 2 tsp. vanilla extract
- 1/4 cup unsweetened almond milk (more if needed)

Instructions :

1. Add everything to a food processor (or blender) except the almond milk.
2. Blend until well combined and scrape down the sides.
3. Slowly add the milk and continue to blend until nice and smooth, adding more milk if needed.
4. Taste and add additional sweetener or chocolate if needed.

Per serving: 14g CARBS, 2g FAT, 4g PROTEIN

Buffalo Chicken Celery Bites

Prep Time	Cook Time	Calories
5min	5 min	80 kcal

Ingredients :

- 2 cups cooked boneless and skinless chicken breast, shredded
- 1 tsp. garlic powder
- 1 tsp. onion powder
- 1/2 tsp. black pepper
- 1/4 cup nonfat Greek yogurt (or mayo or cream cheese)
- 1/4 cup buffalo sauce
- 8 stalks celery

Instructions :

1. Mix together the chicken, garlic powder, onion powder, black pepper, and either Greek yogurt, mayonnaise, or cream cheese, and buffalo sauce.

2. You can also use a combination of Greek yogurt and either mayo or cream cheese for a richer flavor that's still light.

3. Cut the celery ribs into thirds. Stuff with buffalo chicken.

4. Top with blue cheese or ranch dressing.

Per serving: 3g CARBS, 1g FAT, 13g PROTEIN

CROCK POT REFRIED BEAN DIP

Prep Time	Cook Time	Calories
10 min	**2hours**	**68 kcal**

Ingredients :

- 1 can (16 ounces) fat-free refried beans
- ½ cup salsa
- ½ cup fat-free cheddar or Monterey jack cheese
- ½ teaspoon chili powder
- ¼ teaspoon garlic powder
- Optional garnishes: chopped green onion, fresh cilantro

Instructions :

1. Ideal slow cooker size: 1-½-Quart.

2. Combine the refried beans, salsa, cheese, chili powder and garlic powder in your crock pot.

3. Stir well.

4. Cover and cook on LOW for 2 to 3 hours, until the mixture is hot and the cheese is melted. Give the mixture a quick stir every hour or so to check on it's progress.

5. Serve this easy crock pot refried bean dip right from your slow cooker or dump it into a serving dish.

6. If desired, you can doll it up by sprinkling chopped green onion and/or cilantro on top.

7. Serve with corn chips and/or raw vegetables for dipping.

Per serving: Fat 0g, Carbohydrates 11g, Fiber 3.3g, Protein 5.5g

Dessert O Point Weight Loss Meals

| Weight Watcher's Fluff

Prep Time	**Calories**
20 min	**50 kcal**

| Ingredients :

- 2 cups fat free plain yogurt/ fat free Greek yogurt
- 1 packet sugar free jelly / jello crystals or powder (approx 11.5g)
- ½ cup boiling water (¼ pint)
- ½ cup cold water (¼ pint)
- 6 strawberries to decorate - optional

| Instructions :

1. Pour the jelly/jello crystals or powder into a jug and add the boiling water. Stir for a couple of minutes to dissolve.

2. Once the powder has dissolved in the boiling water you can add the cold water and then set it aside to cool for 5 minutes.

3. Pour the yogurt into the bowl of your stand mixer (or if you are using a handheld mixer, into a large bowl). Whisk for 2 - 3 minutes until lots of bubbles are starting to form on the top.

4. Slowly pour the jelly/jello mixture in a steady stream into the yogurt whilst continuing to whisk. Whisk for a further 5 - 10 minutes until the mixture has increased in volume and is light and bubbly.

5. Spoon the mixture into individual ramekins. If you are wanting to turn out the fluff (as in the photograph) coat the inside of individual pudding bowls with a very thin layer of spray oil before spooning the mixture in.

6. Place in the fridge to chill for at least 2 hours until the fluff has set. If you are turning out the fluff, run the tip of a knife around the edge of the pudding bowls before turning out on to a plate. Serve with sliced strawberries.

Per serving: Fat 1 g , Saturated Fat 1 g , Cholesterol 2 mg ,Sodium 66 mg , Potassium 227 mg , Carbohydrates 7 g ,Fiber 1 g , Sugar 7 g , Protein 5 g

| Cheesecake

Prep Time	Cook Time	Calories
10min	**30min**	**72.97kcal**

| Ingredients :

- 3 eggs
- 3 cups non fat greek yogurt I prefer Fage 0%
- 1 small box instant fat free/sugar free cheesecake of vanilla pudding mix
- 1 tbsp imitation vanilla
- 3 tbsp Stevia

| Instructions :

1. Preheat oven to 350 degrees

2. In a medium sized mixing bowl, add eggs, vanilla, and stevia until blended well

3. Add in yogurt and box of pudding until well combined

4. Spray a pie dish or 9 inch spring form pan with non stick cooking spray and pour ingredients in

5. Bake for 30 minutes

6. Let cool for 15-20 minutes before covering with plastic wrap

7. Chill overnight in the refrigerator

Per serving: Carbohydrates: 3.13g | Protein: 9.72g | Fat: 1.86g | Saturated Fat: 0.6g | Cholesterol: 65.13mg | Sodium: 55.93mg | Potassium: 128.52mg | Sugar: 2.7g | Vitamin A: 89.1IU | Calcium: 91.74mg | Iron: 0.34mg

| Lemon Meringue Cookies

Prep Time	Cook Time	Calories
15min	1hour	2 kcal

| Ingredients :

- 2 large Egg whites (at room temperature)
- 1/2 tsp Cream of tartar
- 1 tsp Vanilla extract
- 1 pinch Sea salt
- 1/4 cup Besti Powdered Monk Fruit Allulose Blend

| Instructions :

1. Preheat the oven to 200 degrees F (93 degrees C). Line a large baking sheet with parchment paper.

2. In a large bowl, using a hand mixer at medium speed, beat the egg whites and cream of tartar, until the egg whites get opaque and frothy.

3. Add the salt (if using) and vanilla extract. Increase the speed to high and continue to beat until stiff peaks form.

4. Gradually beat in Besti powdered sweetener.

5. Carefully to avoid breaking down the egg whites, transfer the mixture into a piping bag, which gives the look of classic meringues). Pipe cookies onto the lined baking sheet, spaced about an inch apart.

6. Bake for 1-2 hours, until the keto meringue cookies are firm and release easily from the parchment paper (but don't move them yet!), and before they turn brown. Time will vary depending on the size and thickness of your meringues.

7. When they are done, turn off the oven and prop the door with a wooden spoon. Leave the meringues in the oven this way for at least one hour, until dry and crisp.

Per serving: Fat 0.1g ,Protein 0.3g, Total Carbs 0g, Net Carbs 0g ,Fiber 0g ,Sugar 0.1g

Chocolate Banana Ice Cream

Prep Time	Calories
2 hours	**108 kcal**

Ingredients :

- 3 ripe bananas
- 3 tablespoons unsweetened cocoa powder
- 1 tablespoon raw agave
- Pinch of salt

Instructions :

1. Slice the banana into rounds. Put the rounds in a closed and covered glass container, in the freezer, for at least two hours.

2. Put the bananas in a blender and blend until the banana rounds are finely chopped.

3. Add in the unsweetened cocoa powder, salt, and raw agave. Blend until it is combined and very creamy.

Per serving: Total Fat 1g, Cholesterol 0mg, Sodium 34mg, Carbohydrates 26g ,Fiber 3g ,Sugar 14g ,Protein 2g

Yield : 4

| Banana Soufflé

Prep Time	Cook Time	Calories
5min	**3min**	**336kcal**

| Ingredients :

- 2 bananas
- 2 eggs

| Instructions :

1. Mash bananas with a fork.

2. Add 2 eggs.

3. Mix all well.

4. Bake in the microwave for 3 minutes. Check to see if it is done. If not, cook for 1 minute more.

5. Top with a sprinkle of cinnamon if desired.

Per serving: Carbohydrates: 55g | Protein: 14g | Fat: 9g | Saturated Fat: 3g | Cholesterol: 327mg | Sodium: 127mg | Potassium: 966mg | Fiber: 6g | Sugar: 29g | Vitamin A: 626IU | Vitamin C: 21mg | Calcium: 61mg | Iron: 2mg

| Mini Cheesecakes

Prep Time	**Cook Time**
10min	**30min**

| Ingredients :

- 3 cups plain nonfat Greek yogurt
- 3 eggs
- small box of sugar free fat free pudding mix, cheesecake flavor
- 3 tbsp Splenda (or your favorite sweetener)
- 1 tbsp vanilla extract

| Instructions :

1. Preheat oven to 350ºF. Line a muffin tin with cupcake liners. Lightly spray with nonstick cooking spray.

2. Whisk together all ingredients.

3. Divide batter evenly between the cupcake liners . Bake for 30 minutes.

4. Cool completely at room temperature and then keep chilled.

Strawberry Sorbet

Ingredients :

- 1 banana, sliced and frozen
- 2 cup strawberries, frozen
- 2 tablespoons almond milk
- ½ teaspoon vanilla

Instructions :

1. Place all of the ingredients in a food processor and blend until smooth. The consistency should be like sorbet.

2. Transfer to a freezer-safe container large enough to hold 2 cups, and freeze for at least 3 hours.

3. Scoop with an ice cream scoop and serve cold.

4. Serving size: ½ cup.

Per serving: Calories: 62, Sugar: 8.1g ,Sodium: 0 ,Fat: 0.3g ,Saturated Fat: 0 ,Carbohydrates: 15,9g ,Fiber: 3 ,Protein: .8g

| Frozen Candy Grapes

| Ingredients :

- 2 cups seedless grapes

- 1 Tbsp sugar free powdered drink mix or gelatin mix of your choice

| Instructions :

1. wash grapes

2. separate grapes from stem and put in zipper lock plastic bag

3. add powdered drink mix

4. shake vigorously

5. freeze for at least one hour

6. enjoy, guilt free!

| Two Ingredient Watermelon Ice Cream

Prep Time	Cook Time	Calories
4hours	**10min**	**54kcal**

| Ingredients :

- 3 cups watermelon
- 1/2 cup lite canned coconut milk (or yogurt or sweetened condensed milk)

| Instructions :

1. Freeze the watermelon cuber in a single layer on a piece parchment paper or foil for at least 3-4 hours.

2. When ready to make, add half the watermelon to the food processor and blend until smooth.

3. Scrape down the sides and add the yogurt, coconut milk, or condensed milk.

4. Add the remaining watermelon and blend until smooth and creamy.

5. Eat immediately or freeze for 2-3 hours for a firmer texture. If frozen longer, leave it out for 30 minutes before eating so it can soften up and become creamy.

Per serving: 9g CARBS, 2g FAT, 1g PROTEIN

Made in the USA
Las Vegas, NV
12 March 2024

87076230R00056